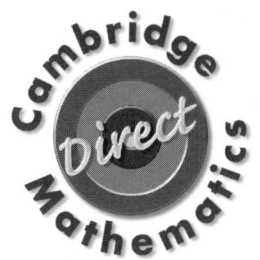

Measures, Shape, Space and Handling Data 4

Solutions

PUBLISHED BY THE PRESS SYNDICATE OF THE UNIVERSITY OF CAMBRIDGE
The Pitt Building, Trumpington Street, Cambridge, United Kingdom

CAMBRIDGE UNIVERSITY PRESS
The Edinburgh Building, Cambridge CB2 2RU, UK
40 West 20th Street, New York, NY 10011-4211, USA
10 Stamford Road, Oakleigh, VIC 3166, Australia
Ruiz de Alarcón 13, 28014 Madrid, Spain
Dock House, The Waterfront, Cape Town 8001, South Africa

http://www.cambridge.org

© Cambridge University Press 2001

First published 2001

Printed in the United Kingdom at the University Press, Cambridge

Typefaces Frutiger, Swift   *System* QuarkXPress 4.1®

A catalogue record for this book is available from the British Library

ISBN 0 521 79827 2 paperback

General editors for Cambridge Mathematics Direct
Sandy Cowling, Jane Crowden, Andrew King, Jeanette Mumford

Writing team for *Measures, Shape, Space and Handling Data 4*
Anne Barber, Salliann Coleman, Sandy Cowling, Pete Crawford,
Jane Crowden, Lorely James, Mary Nathan, Marian Reynolds,
Allison Toogood, Elizabeth Toohig, Fay Turner, Joanne Woodward

The writers and publishers would like to thank the many schools and
individuals who trialled lessons for Cambridge Mathematics Direct.

NOTICE TO TEACHERS
The pages in this publication may be photocopied free of charge for classroom
use within the school or institution which purchases the publication. Worksheets and
photocopies of them remain in the copyright of Cambridge University Press and such
photocopies may not be distributed or used in any way outside the purchasing institution.
Written permission is necessary if you wish to store the material electronically.

Notes

Solutions to textbook and copymaster questions are listed under the
title of the lesson in the teacher's handbook. Lessons are in the same
order as in the teacher's handbook.

Solutions are written in different forms:
- Complete solutions are listed wherever it is useful.
- Facsimiles of completed copymasters are included where this is
  most helpful.
- For open-ended questions and investigations, possibilities are
  indicated through examples where this is helpful.

You can learn most about children's misconceptions by marking
their work with them or discussing incorrect answers after marking.

Solutions may be photocopied (under the conditions detailed above).

Measures

M1.1 Introducing perimeter

TB pages 5–6

★1 a 8 cm + 2 cm + 8 cm + 2 cm = 20 cm
    b 5 cm + 7 cm + 5 cm + 7 cm = 24 cm
    c 7 cm + 1 cm + 7 cm + 1 cm = 16 cm
    d 13 cm + 3 cm + 13 cm + 3 cm = 32 cm
    e 3 cm + 4 cm + 5 cm = 12 cm

A1 a 3 cm + 8 cm + 8 cm = 19 cm
    b 3 cm + 3 cm + 3 cm + 3 cm = 12 cm
    c $1\frac{1}{2}$ cm + 2 cm + 2 cm + $1\frac{1}{2}$ cm + 2 cm = 9 cm
    d 2 cm + 2 cm + 2 cm + 2 cm + 2 cm + 2 cm = 12 cm
    e 4 cm + 4 cm + 4 cm = 12 cm
    f 7 cm + 5 cm + 5 cm + 7 cm + 3 cm = 27 cm
    g $2\frac{1}{2}$ cm + 7 cm + 4 cm + 2 cm = $15\frac{1}{2}$ cm

B1 a Outline drawn around children's own choice of object
    b Estimate of the perimeter of the shape in part a in mm
    c Actual perimeter of the shape in part a in mm

B2 Children repeat B1 for 2 more objects.

M1.3 Metres and kilometres

CM 2

2 a 5000 m   b 6500 m   c 18 000 m
3 a 3 km   b 10 km   c 0.5 km
4 Sam's house is nearest the sea, because a kilometre is shorter than a mile.
5 It will take Sue less time, because 1 km is less than a mile.
6 Children's own 3 questions

M1.4 Fractions and decimals of length measures

TB pages 7–8

A1 a 50 cm   b 170 cm   c 168 cm
    d 25 cm   e 134 cm   f 45 cm
    g 85 cm   h 75 cm   i 125 cm
    j 150 cm

A2 a kilometres (or metres)
    b centimetres (or millimetres)
    c metres (or centimetres)
    d millimetres (or centimetres)
    e centimetres
    f centimetres

B1 Abigail 3500 m, Keisha 2750 m, Oliver 1250 m, Mark 4750 m, Emma 5500 m, Ruben 5080 m, Andrew 4200 m, Megan 3250 m, Beth 2500 m, Sam 1750 m

B2 3500 m, 2800 m, 1300 m, 4800 m, 5500 m, 5100 m, 4200 m, 3300 m, 2500 m, 1800 m

CM 3

Fraction of 1 m	Length in cm
$\frac{1}{2}$ m	50 cm
$\frac{1}{4}$ m	25 cm
$\frac{3}{4}$ m	75 cm
$\frac{1}{10}$ m	10 cm

CM 5

The matching lengths are:
1 km and 1000 m
5 cm and 50 mm
10 mm and 1 cm
5 mm and $\frac{1}{2}$ cm
1 m and 100 cm
500 m and $\frac{1}{2}$ km
3 m and 300 cm
250 m and $\frac{1}{4}$ km
2000 m and 2 km
$\frac{1}{2}$ m and 50 cm

M1.5 Problems using measures of length

TB pages 9–10

A1 The items fit together exactly on a 44 cm × 28 cm table, e.g.

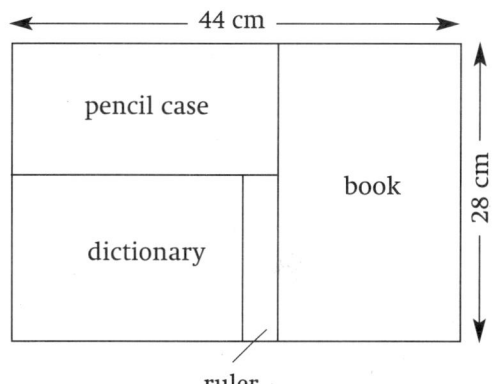

A2 144 cm or 1.44 m

B1 a The easiest way is to extend the table from A1 to a 44 cm × 44 cm table, but square tables with smaller perimeters can be found, e.g. 40 cm × 40 cm.
    b For a 44 cm × 44 cm table, the perimeter is 176 cm. A 40 cm × 40 cm table has a perimeter of 160 cm.

B2 Children's estimate of the height of a table, approximately 70 cm

C1 a Zute and Zolto
    b Zoll and Zono

C2 a The shortest route is: Zute, Zingle, Zono, Zoll, Zolto, Zoth, Zute.
    b The distance for the shortest route is: 64 km + 41 km + 30 km + 115 km + 81 km + 88 km = 419 km

C3 Children's own journeys, with the distances travelled

M2.1 Reading scales
CM 8

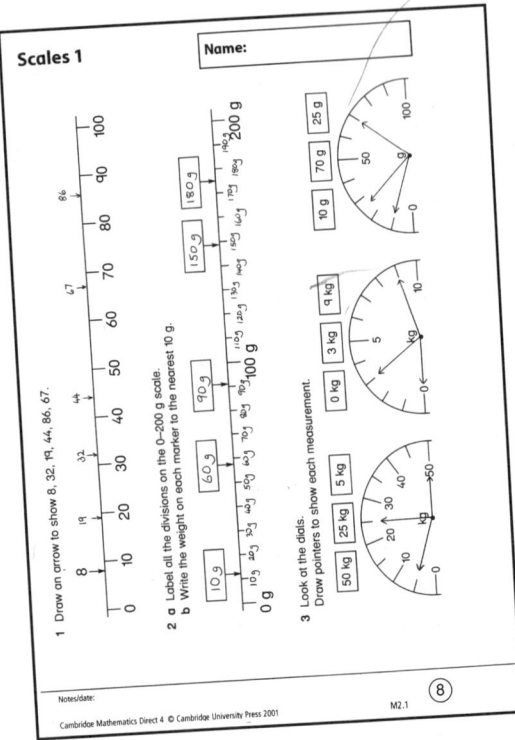

CM 9

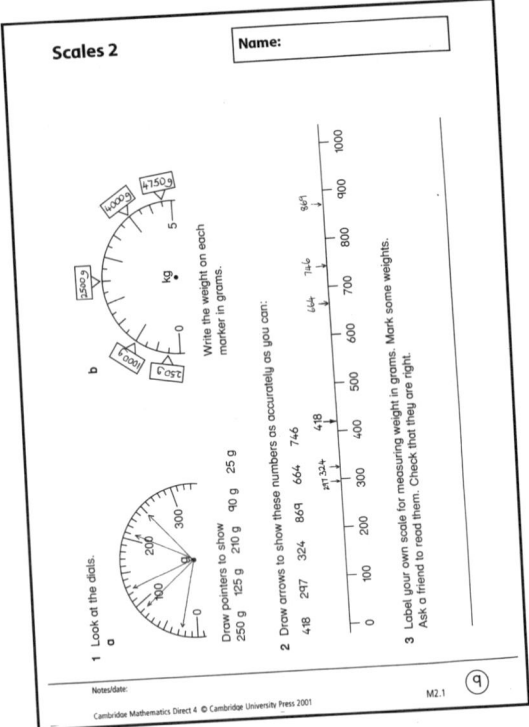

M2.2 Adding and subtracting
TB pages 11–12

A1 a 500 g + 200 g + 200 g = 900 g
    b 200 g + 200 g + 50 g = 450 g
    c 200 g + 100 g + 50 g = 350 g
    d 200 g + 200 g + 200 g + 50 g = 650 g

A2 a 400 g + 250 g = 650 g
    b 350 g – 100 g = 250 g
    c 1 kg – 200 g = 1000 g – 200 g = 800 g

B1 250 g + 150 g + 300 g = 700 g
    She did not have enough potatoes; she was 750 g – 700 g = 50 g short.

B2 a 600 g = 500 g + **100 g**
    b 550 g = **500 g** + **50 g**
    c 850 g = 500 g + 200 g + 100 g + 50 g
    d 800 g = 500 g + 200 g + 100 g

C1 a Any 10 out of:
       50 g, 100 g, 150 g, 200 g, 250 g, 300 g, 500 g, 550 g, 600 g, 650 g, 700 g, 750 g, 800 g
    b 800 g – 50 g = 750 g
    c 350 g, 400 g or 450 g (though these could all be done if you put weights on both sides of the scales)

C2 flour + 100 g = 500 g

M2.3 Halving and doubling

TB pages 13–14

A1 a   400 g self-raising flour
        200 g margarine
        240 g caster sugar
        100 g sultanas
        50 g cherries
        60 g currants
        2 eggs
        4 tablespoons of milk
    b   24 rock cakes

A2 100 g plain chocolate
    25 g margarine
    125 g cereal flakes
    50 g honey

B1 a 900 g   b 1500 g   c 1250 g
    d 400 g   e 250 g, 50 g, 1500 g

C1 a Weigh 100 g + 100 g
    b Weigh 100 g then divide it into 2 equal heaps on the scales, using 1 heap to balance the other.
    c Use 50 g left over from b and add to 100 g + 100 g + 100 g + 100 g

M2.4 Multiplying and dividing

TB pages 15–16

★1 50 g grated cheese
    100 g margarine
    10 g mustard
    300 g plain flour
    water to mix

A1 300 grams plain flour
    15 grams bicarbonate of soda
    30 grams ground ginger
    75 grams margarine
    150 grams soft brown sugar
    60 grams golden syrup
    enough milk to mix to a firm dough

B1 a 4 × 50 g = 200 g
    b 3 × 50 g = 150 g
    c 6 × 50 g = 300 g

C1 a 150 g   b 900 g   c 3000 g
    d 1500 g   e 210 g   f 1400 g
    g 3500 g   h 700 g

C2 8 grapefruit weigh 8 × 250 g = 2000 g. 2000 g ÷ 200 g = 10, so you need ten 200 g masses.

C3 450 g ÷ 50 g = 9
    9 × 3 = **27 'fun-size' chocolate bars**

C4 Oranges weigh 1000 g ÷ 5 = 200 g, apples weigh 600 g ÷ 4 = 150 g, so an orange is heavier by 50 g.

M3.1 Reading scales

TB page 17

A1 a 700 ml lemonade
    b 250 ml water
    c 100 ml orange juice
    d 400 ml cola

B1 CM 11 completed by adding liquid up to the following levels:
    a 250 ml   b 100 ml
    c 750 ml   d 500 ml

C1 CM 11 completed by adding liquid up to the following levels:
    a 800 ml   b 180 ml
    c 0 ml   d 450 ml

M3.2 Adding and subtracting litres and millilitres

TB pages 18–19

★1 a 400 ml + 300 ml = **700 ml**
    b 10 l + 15 l = **25 l**
    c 850 ml − 250 ml = **600 ml**
    d 100 l − 5 l = **95 l**
    e 63 ml + 37 ml = **100 ml**
    f $4\frac{3}{4}$ l − $1\frac{1}{2}$ l = **$3\frac{1}{4}$ l**

B1 a 800 ml   b 400 ml
    c 900 ml   d 600 ml

B2 a 140 ml   b 80 ml

B3 a 300 ml   b 350 ml
    c $12\frac{1}{2}$ l   d $45\frac{1}{5}$ l

C1 Children's own word problems based on the calculations in ★1

CM 12

1   c 500 ml
    d 200 ml + 300 ml = 500 ml

2   c 900 ml
    d $\frac{1}{2}$ l + 400 ml = 900 ml or 500 ml + 400 ml = 900 ml

3 c 450 ml
   d $\frac{3}{4}$ litre − 300 ml = 450 ml or
      750 ml − 300 ml = 450 ml

4 c 550 ml
   d 1 litre − 450 ml = 550 ml or
      1000 ml − 450 ml = 550 ml
   f 300 ml
   g 450 ml − 150 ml = 300 ml

5 c 850 ml
   d 700 ml + 150 ml = 850 ml

M3.3 Halving and doubling litres and millilitres

TB pages 20–21

A1 a $\frac{2}{10}$ litre or 200 ml blackcurrant cordial
       1 litre apple juice
       800 ml water
    b 2 litres boiling water
       4 oranges cut in quarters
       8 lemons cut in quarters
       1 litre sugar syrup
    c $\frac{2}{10}$ litre or 200 ml lime cordial
       100 ml lemon juice
       1 litre grapefruit juice
       $\frac{4}{10}$ litre tonic water
    d 400 ml chocolate syrup
       $1\frac{1}{2}$ litres milk
       600 ml cream
       100 ml mint essence

B1 a 50 ml blackcurrant cordial
       $\frac{1}{4}$ litre apple juice
       200 ml water
    b $\frac{1}{2}$ litre boiling water
       1 orange cut in quarters
       2 lemons cut in quarters
       $\frac{1}{4}$ litre sugar syrup
    c 50 ml lime cordial
       25 ml lemon juice
       250 ml grapefruit juice
       $\frac{1}{10}$ litre or 100 ml tonic water
    d 100 ml chocolate syrup
       375 ml milk
       150 ml cream
       25 ml mint essence

B2 a 250 ml blackcurrant cordial
       $1\frac{1}{4}$ litres apple juice
       1 litre water
    b $2\frac{1}{2}$ litres boiling water
       5 oranges cut in quarters
       10 lemons cut in quarters
       $1\frac{1}{4}$ litres sugar syrup
    c 250 ml lime cordial
       125 ml lemon juice
       $1\frac{1}{4}$ litres grapefruit juice
       $\frac{1}{2}$ litre or 500 ml tonic water
    d 500 ml chocolate syrup
       1 litre 875 ml milk
       750 ml cream
       125 ml mint essence

M3.4 Multiplying litres and millilitres

TB pages 22–23

A1 a 3 × 200 ml = 600 ml
    b 2000 ml ÷ 250 ml = 8, so 8 glasses
    c 4 × 150 ml = 600 ml
    d 3000 ml ÷ 1500 ml = 2, so 2 hot-water bottles
    e 5 × 50 ml = 250 ml

A2 a 5 coffee cups
    b 6 × 300 ml = 1800 ml,
       2000 ml − 1800 ml = 200 ml,
       so 200 ml water left
    c 4 × 340 ml = 1360 ml = 1 litre 360 ml
    d 3 × 1500 ml = 4500 ml,
       5000 ml − 4500 ml = 500 ml,
       so 500 ml water left
    e 13 spoons

C1 a 8 × 2250 ml = 18 000 ml = 18 litres,
       20 l − 18 l = 2 l,
       so 2 litres water left
    b 4 × 750 ml = 3000 ml = 3 l,
       4 l − 3 l = 1 l,
       so 1 litre milk left
    c You can get 13 glasses of wine from a
       2-litre bottle and 5 from a 750 ml bottle.
       So, you can get 8 more glasses from a
       2-litre bottle.
    d 2000 ml ÷ 50 ml = 40, so 40 days, which
       is nearly 6 weeks.
    e 9 buckets; 2 litres will be left in the last
       bucket.

M3.5 Estimating capacity

CM 15

1. Things to measure in litres, e.g. petrol, large bottles of drink, milk, heating oil, paint, kettle capacity... Things to measure in millilitres, e.g. medicine, ink, drinks in cans, cosmetics...
2. Children's own estimates of capacity similar to:
   - a 40 ml
   - b 4 ml
   - c 100 ml
   - d 200 ml
   - e 1 litre
   - f 3 litres
   - g 8 litres
   - h 10 litres

M4.1 Which unit?

TB pages 24–25

A1
- a In any order: mile, kilometre, metre, centimetre, millimetre
- b mile
- c millimetre
- d In order: millimetre, centimetre, metre, kilometre, mile

A2
- a 1000 mm
- b 1000 ml
- c 'Milli' means 'divided into 1000 parts'.

B1
- a grams
- b kilograms
- c metres
- d millimetres
- e millilitres
- f miles or kilometres (or metres)

B2

kilometres	miles
10	6
15	9
20	12
25	15
30	18
35	21

C1
- a Children's own measurements of the capacity of large containers, in litres. Each measurement is converted into pints by doubling.
- b Children find a more accurate way to convert litres to pints. (1 litre is approximately $1\frac{3}{4}$ pints)

M4.2 Using measuring equipment 1

TB page 26

★1
- a 800 ml
- b 1 kg 500 g
- c 2 kg
- d 9 cm
- e 70 cm

★2 Children finish CM 17.

A1
- a 760 ml
- b 1 kg 440 g
- c 2 kg 200 g
- d 87 mm
- e 65 cm

A2
- a 760 ml (or 800 ml)
- b 1 kg 430 g (or 1 kg 400 g)
- c 2 kg 200 g
- d 90 mm (or 100 mm)
- e 70 cm (or 100 cm)

A3 Children finish CM 17.

B1
- a Children do A1 and A2.
- b Children's own pictures of measurements with scales

C1 Children's own scales for measuring length or mass

M4.3 Using measuring equipment 2

TB page 27

★1
- a ruler or tape measure
- b tape measure or metre rule
- c ruler
- d ruler or metre rule
- e ruler
- f ruler
- g tape measure
- h tape measure or metre rule for length, ruler for height

A1 Children say what they could measure and what they would use for each of
- a a cat
- b a person
- c a cake
- d a box of vegetables
- e a pot of yoghurt
- f a teddy bear
- g a house
- h a paddling pool

B1 Children do A1.

B2 Children's own estimate for one of their suggestions for each part of B1

C1 Children find out how people make really large measurements.

M4.4 Solving problems with measures

TB page 28

A1 9 m

A2 200 cm

A3 45 g

A4 4 children

B1 15 cm

B2   190 m

B3   Fifteen 10 g masses

C1   Filling the 500 ml and 100 ml containers twice and then pouring the water into the bucket gives 1200 ml.

C2   5 more coins

M5.1   Finding perimeters

TB pages 29–30

A1   Children measure the perimeter of
a   the top of their table
b   their reading book
c   the board

A2   a   3 cm + 1 cm = 4 cm, double it gives 8 cm
b   10 cm + 7 cm = 17 cm, double it gives 34 cm
c   18 cm + 13 cm = 31 cm, double it gives 62 cm
d   4 m + 50 cm = 4.50 m, double it gives 9 m

A3   Children draw any two rectangles with perimeters of 20 cm:
9 by 1 cm, 8 by 2 cm, 7 by 3 cm
6 by 4 cm or 5 by 5 cm

B1   a   80 cm
b   4 times the length of one side

B2   a   5 × 3 m = 15 m
b   3 × 5 m = 15 m
c   6 × 2 m = 12 m

B3   a   40 cm ÷ 4 = 10 cm
b   32 cm ÷ 4 = 8 cm
c   36 cm ÷ 4 = 9 cm

M5.3   Estimating area

TB pages 31–32

A1   a   Area = 7 square centimetres
b   Area = 8 square centimetres
c   Area = 6 square centimetres
d   Area = 6 square centimetres
e   Area = 8 square centimetres

A2   Children do CM 22.

B1   a   Area = $10\frac{1}{2}$ square centimetres
b   Area = 14 square centimetres
c   Area = $46\frac{1}{2}$ square centimetres

d   Area = 28 square centimetres
e   Area = 22 square centimetres

B2   Children draw 3 letters from their name on squared paper and write the area.

C1   Children find different ways of halving a 5 × 5 pinboard and record their results on CM 23.
Each part must have an area of 8 square centimetres.

CM 22

1   Area above the line = 12 square centimetres
Area below the line = 24 square centimetres

3   9 square centimetres

4   12 square centimetres

M5.4   Comparing area and perimeter

Homework suggestion

Yes. The area of a square of perimeter 28 cm is 49 square centimetres.

M6.1   Calendars and passing time

TB pages 33–34

A1   18 April

A2   3 September

A3   a   6 months   b   26 weeks
c   26 days (27 in some years)
d   Yes, the castle is open on Saturday 16 June.

A4   a   Around 15 May
b   Anytime between the end of June and mid-July

B1   a   7 September
b   20 July   c   17 August
d   They are on the canoe trip up river.

C1   Children plan their own journey and say:
a   where they start
b   where they are going
c   how they will get there
d   how long the journey will take
e   when they will start
f   when they will return
g   Children's own 3 questions about their planned trip

CM 26

1. one millennium = 1000 years
one week = 7 days
one century = 100 years
one year = 12 months or 52 weeks
one fortnight = 2 weeks
one day = 24 hours
one hour = 60 minutes
one minute = 60 seconds

2. 30 days hath September,
April, June and November.
All the rest have 31,
excepting February alone
which has but 28 days clear
and 29 in each leap year.

4. January, March, May, July, August, October, December

M6.3 Analogue clocks

TB pages 35–36

A1

	Bus 1	Bus 2	Bus 3
Town Centre	20 past 10	quarter to 12	half past 2
Water World	20 to 11	5 past 12	10 to 3
Sports Stadium	11 o'clock	25 past 12	10 past 3
Multi-screen Cinema	20 past 11	quarter to 1	half past 3
Bowling Alley	20 to 12	5 past 1	10 to 4
Theme Park	12 o'clock	25 past 1	10 past 4

B1 a 40 minutes   b 10 minutes
   c 10 past 2   d 55 minutes

C1 a Maggy 15 past 2 or quarter past 2
     Ed 12 past 4
     Harry half past 6
     Indira 29 to 8
   b Maggy 23 past 2
     Ed 20 past 4
     Harry 22 to 7
     Indira 21 to 8
   c Maggy 27 past 2
     Ed 24 past 4
     Harry 18 to 7
     Indira 17 to 8
   d Maggy 9 past 2
     Ed 6 past 4
     Harry 24 past 6
     Indira 25 past 7

CM 32

1. b 15 past 9   c 25 past 6
   d 5 past 2

2. a 25 to 3   b 5 to 4
   c 20 to 1   d 10 to 6

3. a 27 past 3   b 8 past 9
   c 16 past 12   d 4 past 8

4. a 13 to 4   b 29 to 2
   c 4 to 5   d 17 to 12

M6.4 Linking digital and analogue time

TB page 37

B1 3 hours

B2 6 hours

B3 Numeracy News, 1 hour 16 minutes

B4 Helpline, 12 minutes

B5 Children choose 3 programmes from the TV guide and add their running times together.

B6 Children's own 2 questions

CM 34

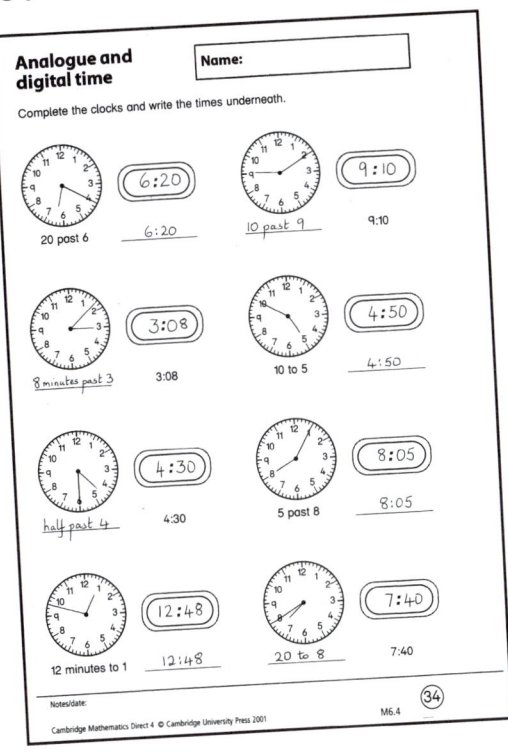

Shape and space

SS1.1 Describing 2-D shapes

TB page 38

A1 Children do CM 36.

B1 a radius   b centre
    c diameter

B2 Children write sentences about
    a the diameter of a circle, e.g. The diameter is a straight line that goes through the centre of the circle and touches the edge of the circle in 2 places.
    b the radius of a circle, e.g. The radius is a straight line that goes from the centre of the circle to its edge.

B3 a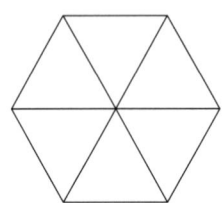

    b Drawing of a hexagon made up of isosceles triangles, e.g
        or

B4 Children draw stars by drawing round
    a an equilateral triangle, e.g
       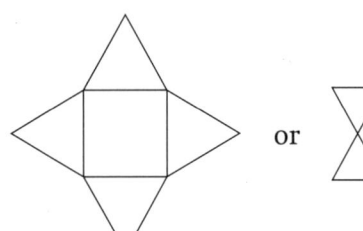

    b an isosceles triangle, e.g
       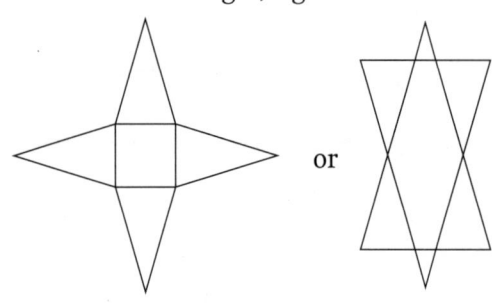

CM 36

4

isosceles	equilateral	ordinary
A, D, G, H	B, F, I	C, E

5 A 10 cm, B 5 cm, D 4 cm, F 7 cm, G 8 cm, H 3 cm, I 2 cm

CM 37

2 Equilateral triangles

4 The corners join together to make a straight line.

6 60°

SS1.2 Polygons

TB page 39

A1 Children sort 6 shapes into polygons and not-polygons and
    a draw round the polygons
    b draw round the not-polygons

A2

Number of sides	Name of shape
7	heptagon
5	pentagon
3	**triangle**
1	circle
8	octagon
6	**hexagon**

C1 a Children draw round an equilateral triangle, square, regular pentagon, regular hexagon, regular heptagon, regular octagon.
    b The square's angles are bigger than the triangle's angles.
    c The angles in a regular polygon are bigger as the number of sides increases.

SS1.3 Making polygons

TB pages 40–41

★1 a Children make a triangle on a pinboard.
    b Drawing of children's own triangle on CM 71

★2 a Children make the largest possible triangle on a pinboard.
    b Drawing of the triangle in part a on CM 71

★3 a Children make the smallest possible triangle on a pinboard.
b Drawing of the triangle in part a on CM 71

★4 a Children make as many more different triangles as they can.
b Drawings of the triangles in part a on CM 71

B1 Children cut a quadrilateral, hexagon, triangle and square from folded pieces of paper, e.g.

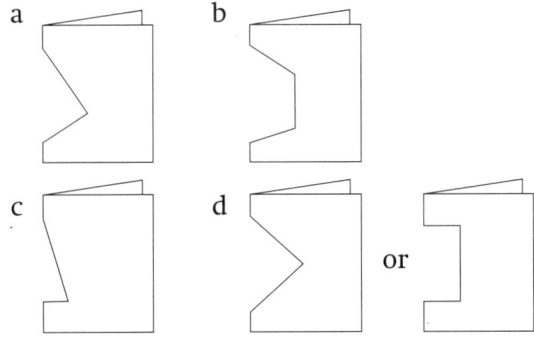

B2 Children stick their shapes from B1 in their books and draw in lines of symmetry.

B3 Children do CM 38.

C1 a–d Children make and draw squares on CM 71.
e 5 squares
f 4 lines of symmetry
g 4 lines of symmetry

CM 38

1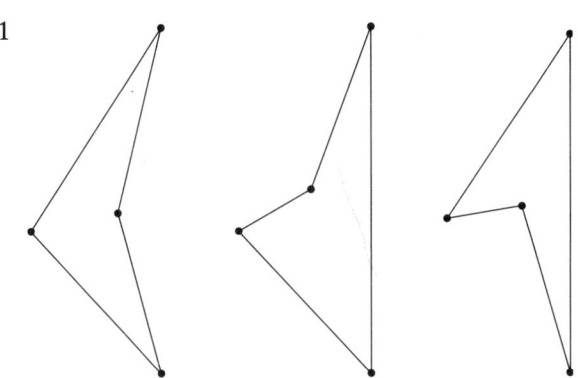

SS1.4 Recognising patterns and relationships

Homework suggestion
A 10-sided star shape can be made by overlapping 2 pentagons. It cannot be made by drawing diagonals without lifting your pencil.
10 triangles make up the points of the star.

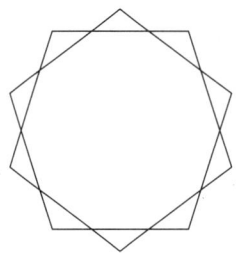

SS2.1 Prisms

TB page 42

B1

Shape of end face	Number of edges of end face
square	4
hexagon	6
octagon	8
triangle	3
heptagon	7
pentagon	5

B2

Number of edges of end face	Number of faces altogether in the prism
4	6
6	8
8	10
3	5
7	9
5	7

B3 23 + 2 = 25 faces

C1

Number of edges of end face	Number of edges altogether in the prism
4	12
6	18
8	24
3	9
7	21
5	15

C2 $17 \times 3 = 51$ edges

C3 The number of vertices altogether is twice the number of edges of the end face.

SS2.2 Polyhedra

TB page 43

- A1 Children play shape dominoes.
- A2 a square-based pyramid or tetrahedron
  b cube
  c pentagonal prism
  d cone
  e hemi-sphere
- A3 The square-based pyramid, cube, pentagonal prism and tetrahedron are all polyhedra.
- B1 a Children sort 3-D shapes into polyhedra and not-polyhedra.
  b Children sort 3-D shapes into polyhedra and not-polyhedra, 4 or more vertices and fewer than 4 vertices.
  c Children sort their shapes in 2 more ways of their own choice.

SS2.3 Nets of 3-D shapes

TB page 44

- B1 a cube b triangular prism
  c square-based pyramid d cuboid
  e cylinder f cone
- B2 Children explain how they knew what shapes the nets made in B1.

CM 40

A and B are nets for a tetrahedron.

SS2.4 Visualising shapes

TB pages 45–46

- A1 a 11 cubes b 8 cubes
  c 8 cubes d 14 cubes
- A2 a Children make shapes.
  b 11 cubes, 8 cubes, 8 cubes, 14 cubes
- C1 Children make models.

SS2.5 Making polyhedra

CM 42

3-D shape	Square faces	Triangular faces	Circular faces	Rectangular faces	Curved faces
tetrahedron	0	4	0	0	0
cylinder	0	0	2	0	1
triangular prism	0	2	0	3	0
cuboid	0 (or 2)	0	0	6 (or 4)	0
square-based pyramid	1	4	0	0	0
hemi-sphere	0	0	1	0	1
cube	6	0	0	0	0
sphere	0	0	0	0	1
cone	0	0	1	0	1

SS3.1 Classifying and sorting 2-D and 3-D shapes

TB pages 47–48

- ★1 Children make models.
- A1 a Children build model.
  b Children describe model for their partner to build.
  c Children compare models.
- C1 a 5 lines of symmetry
  b 3 lines of symmetry
  c 1 line of symmetry
  d no lines of symmetry
  e no lines of symmetry
  f 6 lines of symmetry
  g 7 lines of symmetry
- C2 Shapes a, b, c, f and g (all regular) have lines of symmetry; shapes d and e (irregular) have no lines of symmetry.
- C3 Children write 3 sentences about lines of symmetry and 2-D shapes, for instance: If a polygon is regular, it will have lines of symmetry... The number of lines of symmetry will equal the number of sides of the shape...
  (NB: irregular shapes can have some lines of symmetry.)
- C4 10 lines of symmetry

SS3.2 Investigating shapes

TB page 49

A1 a Children's own picture using 2-D shapes
    b Children describe picture for partner to draw.
    c Children say whether their partner's drawing under instruction turned out like the one being described.

B1 a Children give any 5 prisms as examples.
    b Children give any 5 pyramids as examples.
    c Children give any 5 regular polygons as examples.

B2 Children's own sentences to explain why the 3 statements in B1 are true.

SS4.1 Recognising line symmetry

CM 45

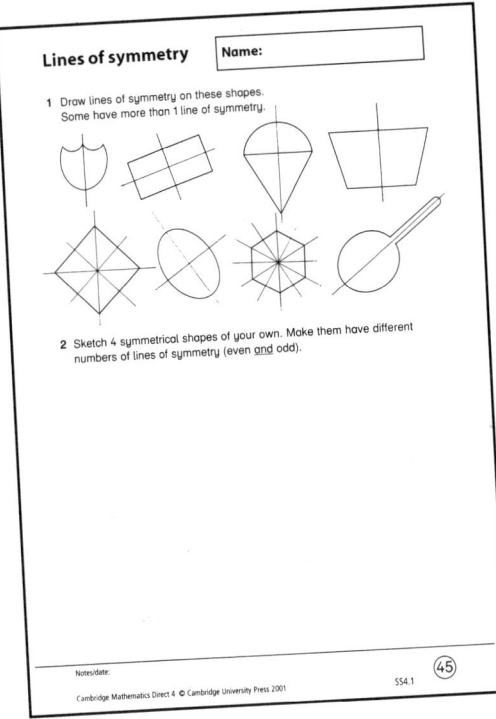

SS4.2 Making reflections

CM 46

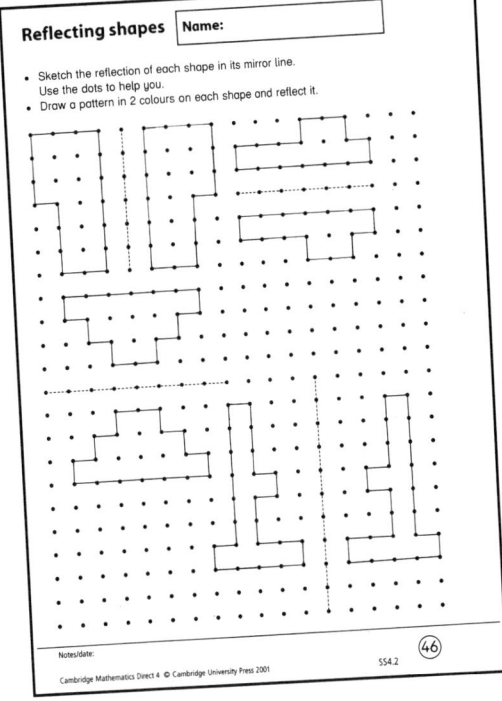

CM 47

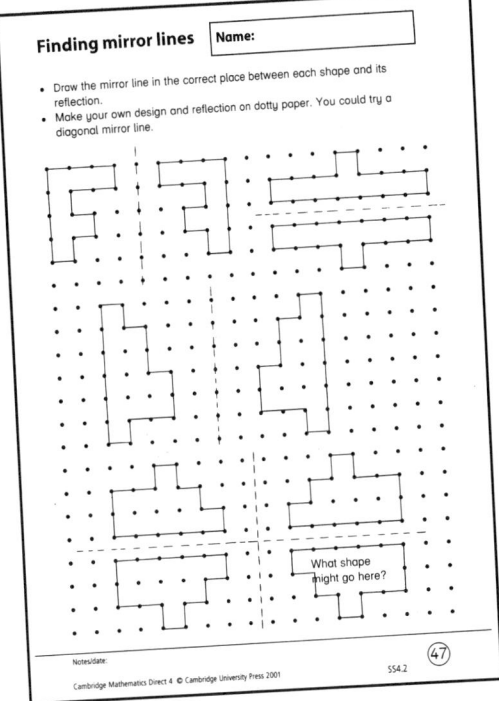

SS5.1 Position and co-ordinates

TB page 50

A1 a The Red Pig
    b Ashak Rainforest
    c Galleon Lake
    d Carib Village
    e Hangman's Rock

A2 a Zantu Village
    b Zantu Rainforest
    c Pirate Camp
    d Sunken Treasure
    e Eagle Rock

B1

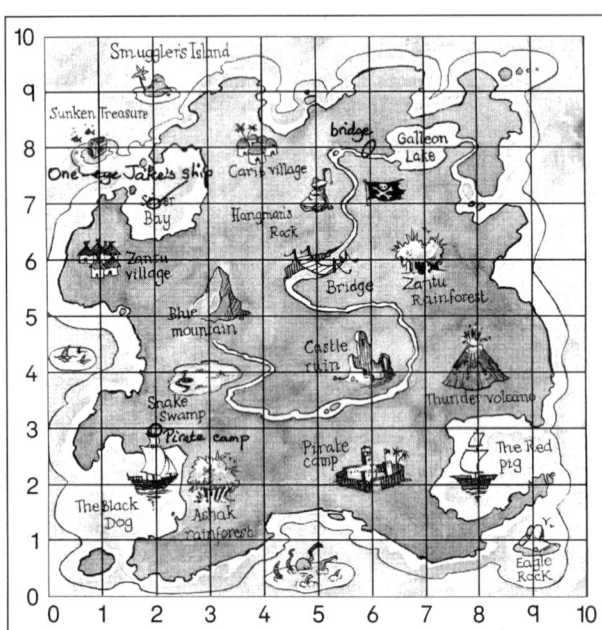

C1 a Children's own map on CM 49
    b Children list everything on their map, giving co-ordinates.

SS5.2 Using co-ordinates

TB page 51

A1 a Carib Village (4, 8)
    b Pirate Camp (6, 2)
    c Ashak Rainforest (3, 2)
    d Zantu Rainforest (7, 6)
    e Smugglers' Island (2, 9)
    f Galleon Lake (7, 8)
    g The Red Pig (8, 2)
    h Blue Mountain (3, 5)
    i Thunder Volcano (8, 4)
    j Hangman's Rock (5, 7)

B1 Children design their own island on CM 50 and give the co-ordinates of 10 features.

C1 Children's own name in co-ordinates using:
    A (2, 3)   B (1, 5)   C (4, 5)
    D (5, 3)   E (6, 1)   F (1, 1)
    G (5, 5)   H (2, 4)   I (4, 2)
    J (2, 2)   K (3, 5)   L (4, 1)
    M (0, 0)   N (5, 2)   O (1, 3)
    P (2, 5)   Q (3, 4)   R (6, 0)
    S (0, 4)   T (3, 3)   U (0, 2)
    V (3, 0)   W (5, 4)   X (3, 6)
    Y (6, 3)   Z (3, 2)

C2 Children's own message written in co-ordinates.

SS5.3 Describing and following directions

TB pages 52–53

A1 a south   b north-east

A2 a Go south to (8, 2).
    b Go north to (3, 5).
    c Go east to (7, 8).
    d Go west to (5, 6).
    e Go north-east to (5, 7).
    f Go north-west to (3, 5).
    g Go south-west to (1, 8).
    h Go south-east to (9, 1).

B1 a Children's own route from The Red Pig at (8, 2) to the Jolly Roger flag at (6, 7) on CM 48
    b Directions for the route in part a
    c List of landmarks passed in part a, with co-ordinates

C1 a Children hide treasure on CM 48
    b Children's choice of starting place
    c Children's directions to the treasure, passing 3 features

SS6.1 Measuring angles in degrees

TB pages 54–55

A1 a Dodgems   b Roundabout
    c Coconut Shy

A2 a 45°   b 90°   c 180°

B1

Start	Turn	End
Hoopla	clockwise 45°	Roundabout
Roundabout	anti-clockwise 90°	**Dodgems**
Win a goldfish	clockwise 180°	**Hoopla**
Coconut shy	clockwise 45°	**Dodgems**
Ghost train	anti-clockwise 180°	**Dodgems**
Arcade machines	anti-clockwise one right angle	**Hoopla**
Big wheel	clockwise 360°	**Big wheel**

B2

Start	Turn	End
Hoopla	**anti-clockwise 45°**	Dodgems
Coconut shy	clockwise three right angles	Win a goldfish
Coconut shy	clockwise 180°	**Arcade machines**
Big wheel	**clockwise one right angle or 90°, or anti-clockwise three right angles**	Dodgems
Win a goldfish	anti-clockwise 45°	Ghost train

B3 a west b south-east
    c south d north-west

B4 Coconut shy

C1 Dodgems

C2 Arcade machines

C3 Children's own questions

SS6.2 Ordering angles
CM 51

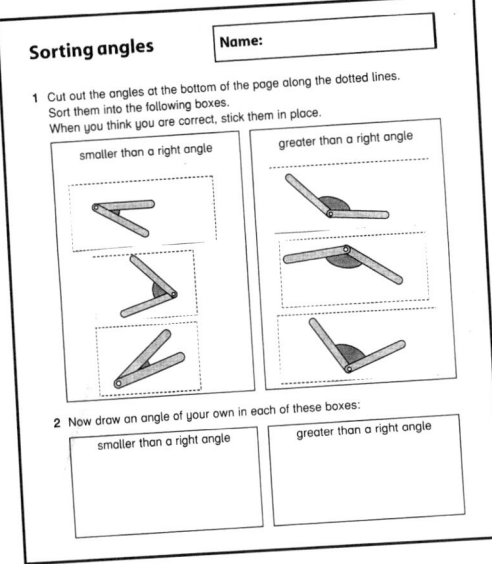

CM 52

1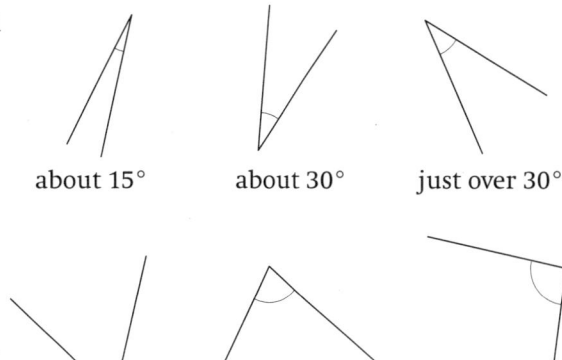

about 15°   about 30°   just over 30°

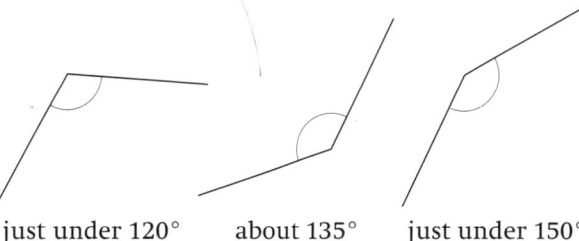

about 60°   between 60° and 90°   just over 90°

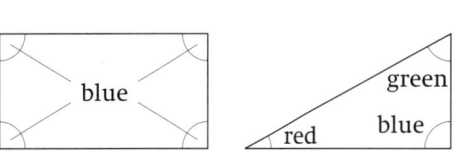 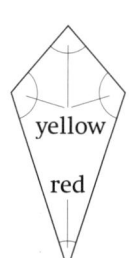

just under 120°   about 135°   just under 150°

2   Children's own angles greater than 45° but smaller than 90°

3

SS6.3 Using a set square
CM 53

1   a 45°   b 90°   c 30°
    d 60°   e 60°   f 90°

2   Children draw angles of
    a 30°   b 45°
    c 60°   d 90°

SS6.4 Making and measuring turns
TB page 56

A1 a 90°   b 60°   c 120°

B1 Children do CM 54.

B2 a 45° (anti-clockwise)
    b 135° (clockwise)

C1 a 60°   b 180°   c 120°
    d 300° clockwise (or 60° anti-clockwise)
    e 240° anti-clockwise (or 120° clockwise)

C2 Children investigate dials with 5, 10 or more settings. To find the number of degrees between each setting, divide 360° by the number of settings, for instance:

Number of settings	Degrees between settings
5	72
10	36
12	30
15	24

CM 54

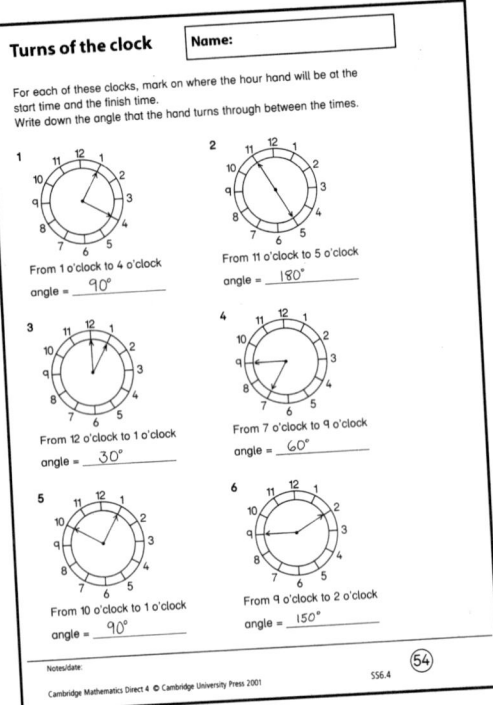

Handling data

HD1.1 Tallying
TB page 57

B1 a–b Children roll 2 dice 50 times and record their results on CM 55.
    c Children's own observations about their results
    d Children explain why their most common total appeared so often. It is likely to be 7 (or close to this) as this total can be made the most ways: 1 + 6, 2 + 5, 3 + 4, 4 + 3, 5 + 2, 6 + 1

C1 a Children's choice of 5 words that they think will appear often in their reading book
    b Children draw a tally chart for their 5 words.
    c Children read 5 pages of their book and complete their tally chart.
    d Children's own observations
    e The frequencies would approximately double.

HD1.2 Making pictograms
TB page 58

★1 a Children's own pictogram, using a symbol that represents 2 fish, showing:
2 lion fish (1 symbol)
3 flying fox fish (1½ symbols)
6 angelfish (3 symbols)
8 clown fish (4 symbols)
    b **Lion fish** is the least common fish.
There are **6** more clown fish than lion fish.
There are **2** times as many angelfish as flying fox fish.

C1 a Children's own pictogram showing:
9 violet soldiers
3 peacock rock cod
24 convict surgeons
18 blue fin jacks
42 black footed clowns
54 bird wrasses
45 two spot red snappers
15 reef lizards
Pictogram includes children's own choice of how many each symbol represents.
    b Children's own 4 sentences about the data

HD1.3 Using charts and tables
TB pages 59–61

★1 a The most popular snack was **fruit**.
    b The least popular snack was **buns**.
    c They sold **53** items.

★2 a Children's own observations about the data
    b Assuming sales on Tuesday will be the same as on Monday:

Snack	Amount
buns	7
brownies	12
raisins	10
fruit	13
drinks	11

A1 a Assault course and zip wire
    b 13 children
    c 9 more children
    d Children's own opinion on why only a few children want to try archery

B1 Children's own suggestions on how the cook should prepare the eggs according to the data.
(Almost everyone likes fried eggs, so this would be a good suggestion, or perhaps cook could offer a choice.)

B2 a 110 visits   b 29 visits
    c The pigs, by 9 visits
    d Children suggest which new animals the staff should get, according to the data. As hens and ducks are the least popular of the current selection of animals, they should advise against getting swans. Pigs and goats are popular, so cows and calves would be a good suggestion.

C1 a Mon   35
Tues   25
Wed   40
Thur   35
Fri   40
Sat   50
Sun   55
    b A sensible suggestion would be to have 5 team leaders available for each weekday and 7 for Saturday and Sunday.

HD2.1 Reading bar charts

TB pages 62–63

A1 a February, March, May and July
    b June and September
    c 8 hours

A2 a 1 August
    b 1 January, 1 December
    c December

B1 a Cairo (it had 10 hours of sunshine, St Lucia had 9 hours)
    b Cairo (it had 7 hours, St Lucia had 8 hours)
    c The bar charts indicate that Cairo had the sunniest time, sometime in June or July. The Cairo bar chart peaks at this time, with 12 hours of sunshine on 1 June and 1 July.
    d The hours of sunshine in St Lucia are fairly consistent throughout the year. Cairo is least sunny in January and December and most sunny in June and July. The number of hours of sunshine increases/decreases steadily between these extremes.

B2 a St Lucia 30°C, Cairo 25°C, Moscow 10°C, London 10°C
    b Children's own questions about the bar chart

C1 Children draw a frequency table and a bar chart (on CM 59), for their own choice of data.

C2 a Children draw more bar charts for the data in C1, with different scales on the vertical axes.
    b Children's own thoughts on which scale works best and why

HD2.2 Making bar charts

Pupil activities

A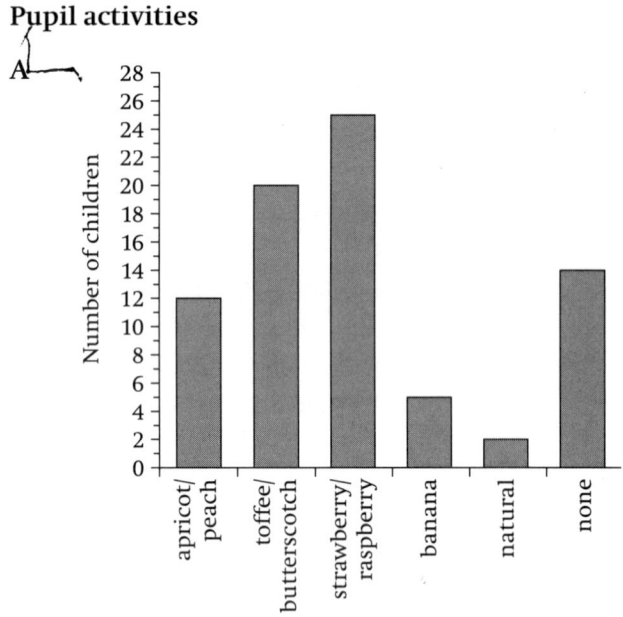

B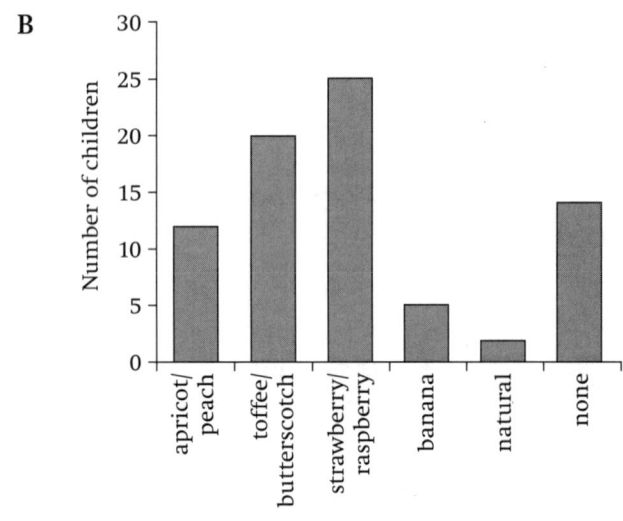

HD2.3 Interpreting bar charts

TB pages 64–66

★1 a

Whether books are brilliant	Number of children
not sure	8
no	6
yes	16

b

Books mostly from	Number of children
school	80
home	60
library	70

A1 a

Best-liked books	Number of children
fact	5
story	12
poetry	11
picture	2

b

Children who read comics	Number of children
never	5
sometimes	20
every week	45
every day	15

c

Whether children would like a book	Number of children
don't know	150
no	70
yes	120

d

Poems that ...	Number of children
are funny	19
tell a story	5
make you think	6

A2 a u   b o
    c 30 + 60 + 20 + 35 + 11 = 156
    d e appeared most frequently. It appears in lots of common words like 'the'.
    e Children's own estimate for the number of words in the paragraph. Many words have 1 or 2 vowels, so about 100 words is a reasonable estimate.

B1 a August   b 20 cm
    c Months that had the same amount of rainfall are: January and May, February and March, June and November, July and September.
    d 15 cm

B2 a June   b 15 cm
    c February d 6 cm

C1 a 6 cm   b July
    c St Lucia (as it has at least as much, and usually more, rain in every month)

C2 Children's own 5 questions

HD3.1 Venn diagrams

TB pages 67–69

★1 a Children make Venn diagram.
    b Children sort shapes.
    c

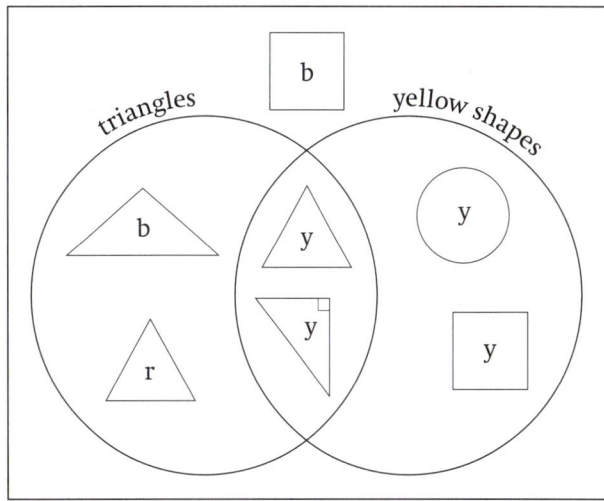

    d red and blue triangles

A1 a Instruments

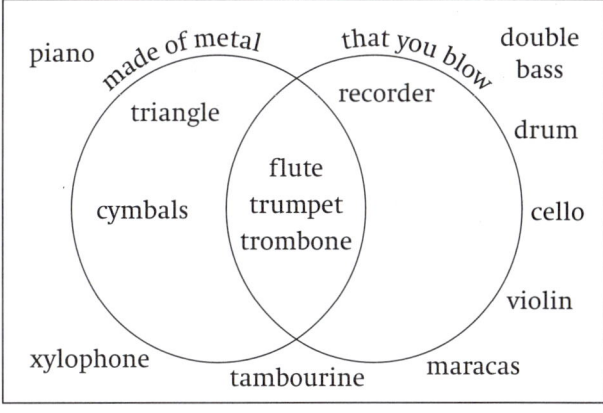

    b The recorder is blown and not made of metal.
    c xylophone

A2 a Children sort flat shapes and draw a Venn diagram.
    b Children name one of the shapes on their diagram and explain why it belongs where they drew it.

B1 a A is the set of **triangles**.
    b right-angled triangle
    c The hexagon goes outside the 2 circles; the other 2 shapes go in the 'with a right angle' circle, outside the overlap.

C1   a

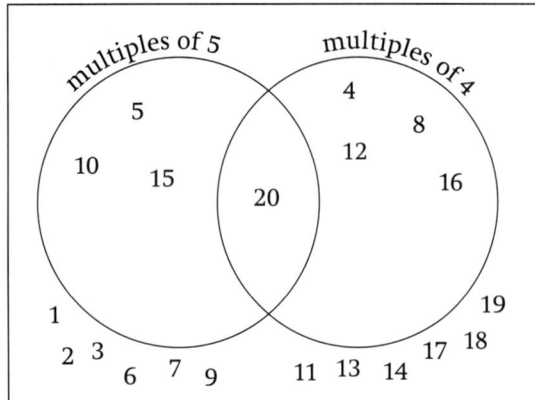

Numbers 1 to 20

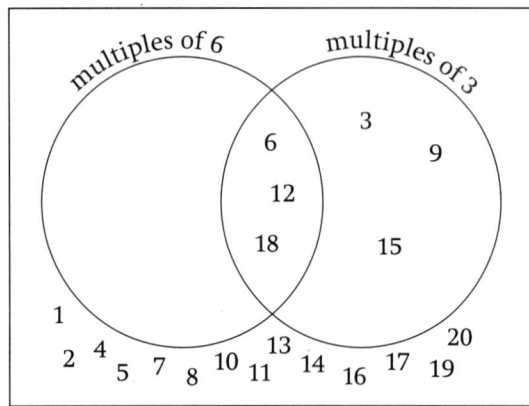

Numbers 1 to 20

   b   **20** is a multiple of 4 and a multiple of 5.
       3, 9, 15 are multiples of 3 but not
       multiples of 6.
   c   Children's own choice of sorting, which
       leaves one part of the Venn diagram
       empty, e.g. multiples of 2 and multiples
       of 4

C2   Children's own choice of sorting

HD3.2   Carroll diagrams

TB page 70

B1   a   50 and 30   b   24 and 48
     c   35 and 45   d   49 and 27

     e   Children's own choice of 2 numbers for
         each of:
         even and divisible by 5
         even but not divisible by 5
         not even but divisible by 5
         not even and not divisible by 5

B2   a   box 3   b   box 1   c   box 2   d   box 4

C1   a   There is a net in football, but not in
         rugby.
     b   Cricket goes in box 2, netball and
         basketball in box 1 and fencing in box 4.
     c

	bat	no bat
net		football tennis badminton ice hockey
no net	rounders	rugby darts running

CM 61

1

	has 31 days	does not have 31 days
summer	July August	June
not summer	January March May October December	February April September November

2   a

	rides a bicycle	does not ride a bicycle
goes swimming	Gareth	Sophie
does not go swimming	Adam	Kuljit

     b   Children add 2 friends' names to the
         Carroll diagram in part a.
     c   Children's own position on the Carroll
         diagram in part a.

HD3.3   Interpreting sorting diagrams

TB pages 71–72

★1   a   Mrs Brown and Connor
     b   Rebecca

A1   a   Ryan, Jake and Rebecca
     b   Tom and Rebecca

A2 a

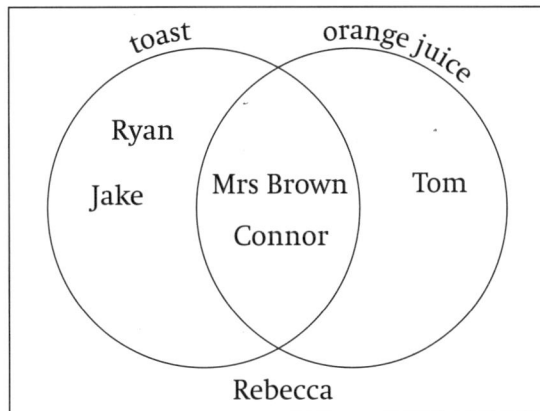

The Browns

b Rebecca does not belong in the circles because she has no toast and no orange juice.

B1

	lives in water	does not live in water
lays eggs	turtle fish	bird snake
does not lay eggs	dolphin whale	giraffe monkey

B2 a The insects are:
wasp, bee, dragonfly, earwig, butterfly, ladybird.
The creatures that can fly are:
wasp, bee, bat, dragonfly, butterfly, ladybird, blackbird, robin.

b Children's choice of Venn diagram or Carroll diagram:

	can fly	cannot fly
insects	wasp bee dragonfly butterfly ladybird	earwig
not insects	bat blackbird robin	snail spider mouse frog

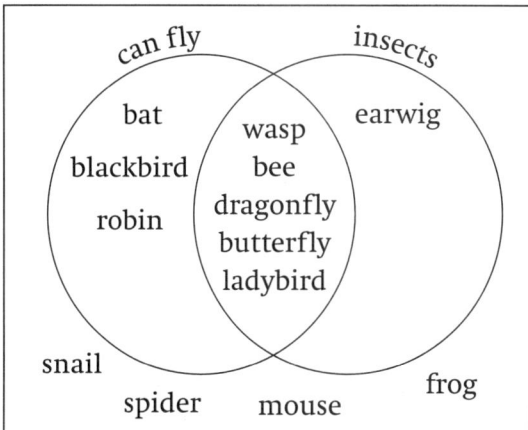

C1 Children add their own choice of creatures to their diagram for B2.

C2 Children discuss which diagram is best for different sorting questions.

Assessment

CM 63   Length

1. 5 mm   10 cm
   30 mm   1000 m
   100 cm   750 m
   172 cm   1000 mm

2. 4000 m   80 mm
   350 cm   220 mm

3. Grandad's house

4. 20 m

5. For example, one of the following rectangles:
   9 by 1 m
   8 by 2 m
   7 by 3 m
   5 by 5 m
   Other shapes are possible.

CM 13   Doubles capacity cards

8000 ml, 4000 ml (twice), 2000 ml, 1000 ml (twice), 900 ml, 800 ml, 700 ml, 600 ml, 500 ml (twice), 450 ml, 400 ml, 350 ml, 300 ml (twice), 250 ml (twice), 200 ml (twice), 150 ml, 100 ml (twice)

CM 64   Flat shapes

not polygons   i, k, q
regular polygons   c, e, n, o, v
isosceles triangles b
pentagons   g, n, s

For a flat shape to be a polygon it must have all its sides straight.
Regular polygons have all sides equal and all angles equal.
Isosceles triangles have 2 sides equal.
Pentagons are polygons with 5 sides.

The following have 2 or more right angles:
c   square
d   rectangle
g   pentagon
j   hexagon
r   octagon
s   pentagon

The following have 1 line of symmetry only:
b   isosceles triangle
g, s   pentagons
k, q   semi-circles
l, r   octagon
p   quadrilateral

CM 39   Shape dominoes

The following are polyhedra:
pyramid
cube
cuboid
tetrahedron
triangular prism

The following are not polyhedra:
cylinder
sphere
hemi-sphere
cone

CM 65   2-D and 3-D shapes

	2-D shape			3-D shape			Name of shape
1	✔	✔	✘	✔	✘	✘	✘	equilateral triangle
2	✘	✘	✘	✘	✔	✔	✘	triangular prism
3	✔	✘	✘	✘	✘	✘	✘	quadrilateral
4	✘	✘	✘	✘	✘	✘	✘	cone
5	✘	✘	✘	✘	✔	✔	✘	cuboid
6	✔	✔	✘	✔	✘	✘	✘	heptagon

CM 66   Angles

1. A quarter turn measures **90°** or 1 **right angle**.
   A half turn measures **180°** or 2 **right angles**.
   A whole turn measures **360°** or 4 **right angles**.
   Half a right angle is **45°**.

2. $a \approx 50°$ (less than 60°, greater than 45°)
   $b \approx 35$ (less than 45° greater than 30°)
   $c \approx 95°$ (greater than 90°)

3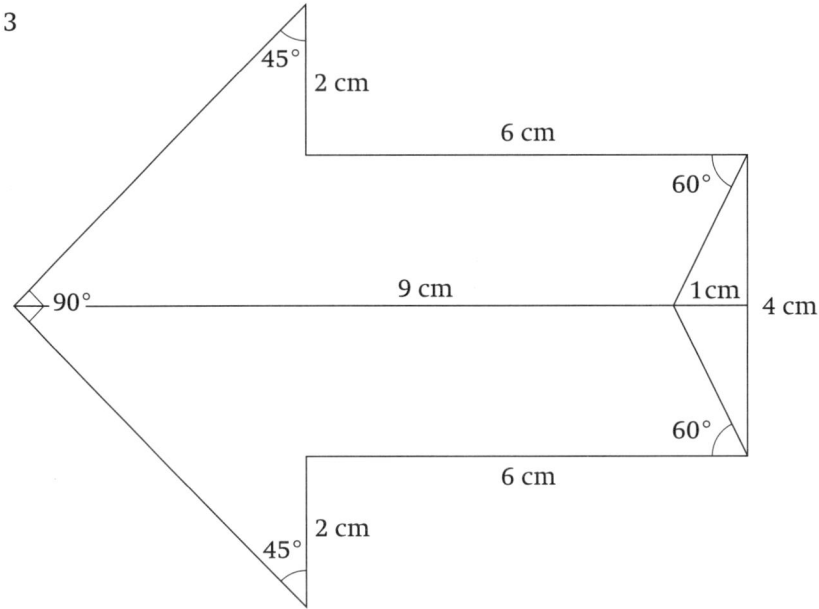

CM 67 Using diagrams

Pet	Tally	Total
cats	|||	3
dogs	|||| |||| ||	12
rabbits	|||	3
guinea pigs	||||		6
hamsters	|||	3

Children draw a pictogram.

1   Children's choice of how many pets each symbol represents (3 would work well for this data.)

2   Children's reason for choice of number

3   6

4   dogs

CM 68 Animal sorting

For example:

animals

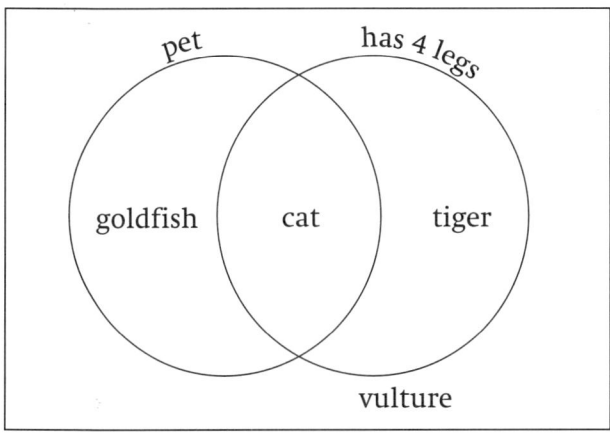